W9-DAU-604

PICTURE-PERFECT
GOLF

JUN '06

OCT 1998

PICTURE-PERFECT GOLF

The 100 Most Common Golf Mistakes and How to Correct Them

Dr. Gary Wiren

PGA Master Professional

with Dawson Taylor

CB

CONTEMPORARY BOOKS

Library of Congress Cataloging-in-Publication Data

Wiren, Gary.
    Picture-perfect golf : the 100 most common golf mistakes and
how to correct them / Gary Wiren with Dawson Taylor.
        p.   cm.
    Includes index.
    ISBN 0-8092-2918-8
    1. Golf.   I. Taylor, Dawson   II. Title.
GV965.W726   1998
796.352—dc21
                                            97-42183
                                            CIP

Cover design by Todd Petersen
Cover photograph by Carlisle Photography, Inc.
Interior design by Jeanette Wojtyla

Published by Contemporary Books
An imprint of NTC/Contemporary Publishing Group, Inc.
4255 West Touhy Avenue, Lincolnwood (Chicago), Illinois 60646-1975 U.S.A.
Copyright © 1998 by Gary Wiren and Dawson Taylor
Manufactured in the United States of America
International Standard Book Number: 0-8092-2918-8

18   17   16   15   14   13   12   11   10   9   8   7   6   5   4   3   2   1

Contents

A Word from the Author

Golf is a wonderful, challenging game. But it can also be a frustrating game, particularly when you continue to make mistakes and don't know how to correct them. When I hear, "I'm hitting the ball terribly and I don't have the slightest idea what to do!" I know it is the cry of a clearly distressed golfer who needs help.

We have all had that hopeless feeling at one time or another. In just such instances a correct thought, idea, or picture could have put us straight. That's why visually enhanced suggestions can help your game.

As an international teacher of golf, I have been privileged to work with and watch the world's best teaching professionals demonstrate their skills in correcting golfers' errors. In this book I present that information in a simple and straightforward manner. If you follow the techniques I have outlined in the following pages and take the time to conscientiously practice the shots that give you the most trouble—even if it's only for 10 minutes a session, three sessions a week—you'll see a noticeable difference in your game and enjoy the results.

Gary Wiren, Ph.D.
Master Teacher, PGA National Golf Club
    Resort and Spa
Palm Beach Gardens, Florida
"Home of the PGA of America"

The Grip

A good definition of an effective grip is "*two hands working as one.*" One hand should not greatly dominate the other. The tendency is for the trailing hand to dominate the lead hand—for most golfers the right hand will dominate the left.[1] This situation is caused partly by the nature of the swing and partly because the right hand is stronger. To assist in balancing the roles of each hand, the player must make certain accommodations in the grip. The left-hand grip, for example, is in the palm and fingers; the right-hand grip is in the fingers only, to help equalize its dominance. The little finger of the right hand is lapped over or interlocked with the index finger of the left, not only to help the hands work as a unit, but also to take away some of the excessive right-hand leverage action and to balance the individual role of each hand.

The degree to which the hands rotate in the grip is most often related to a golfer's ability to return the face of the club to a square position. Physically weaker players need more clockwise rotation so the Vs made by the thumb and index finger of each hand point more toward the right shoulder than the chin. Physically stronger players will generally place their hands so the Vs point more toward the chin than the right shoulder.

[1] The right-handed swing is the model in this book. Left-handers should merely adapt the advice to suit their own swing.

Grip *(Left Hand)*

Mistake: The grip in the left hand should not run across the palm in the fashion shown. When it does, the butt end comes out above the heel pad toward the wrist, causing loss of left-hand grip control.

Correction: The grip should run more across the roots of the fingers, with the butt end coming out below the heel pad of the left hand. This grip allows the little finger to encircle the grip securely.

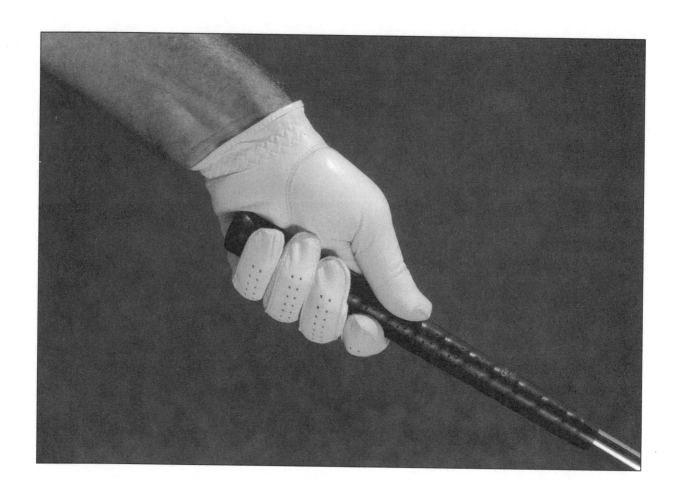

Grip *(Left Hand)*

Mistake: Gripping the club with the left hand extended beyond the butt end of the club causes some loss of grip control during the swing.

Correction: Grip the club in the left hand so that the butt end extends past the heel pad.

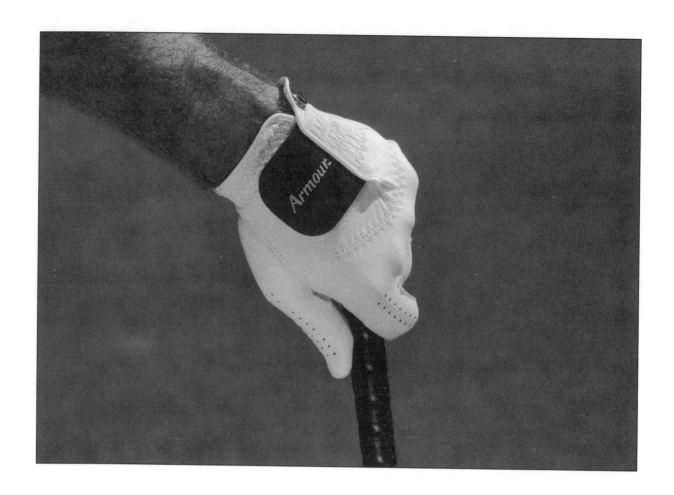

Grip *(Left Hand)*

Mistake: When you have gripped the club over the butt end, you won't be able to see the end when looking at the back of your hand.

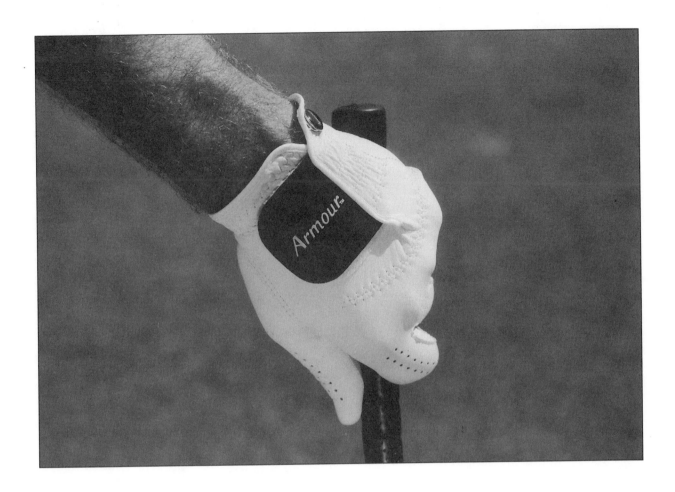

Correction: When your grip is at the correct length, you will be able to see the butt end of the club.

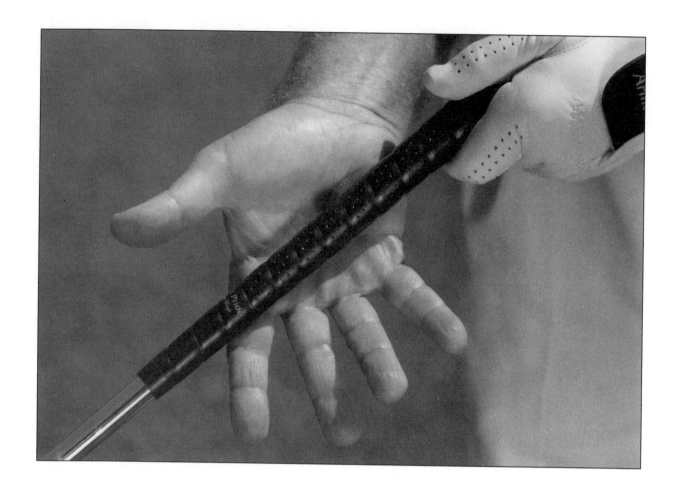

Grip *(Right Hand)*

Mistake: Gripping the club like a hammer too far in the palm of the right hand is a major destroyer of a swing's motion. Such a grip causes the ligaments and tendons across the wrist joint to tighten and reduces clubhead speed.

Correction: Place the right-hand grip in the fingers. This grip may not feel strong, but it eases the grip pressure and assists in producing greater clubhead speed.

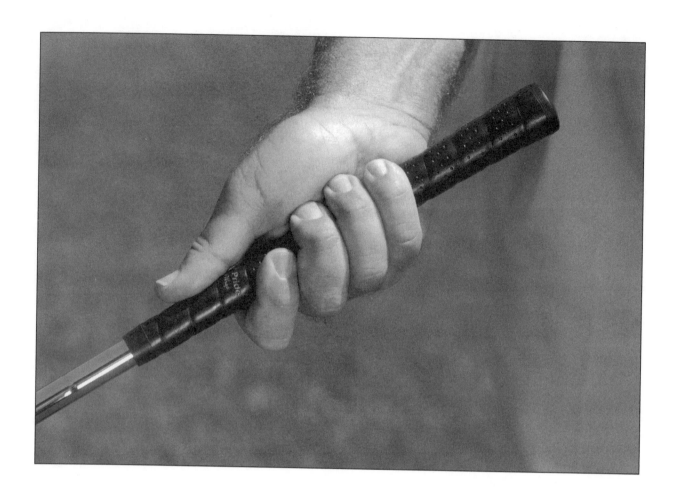

Grip *(Right Hand)*

Mistake: This grip will kill release. It is too much in the palm.

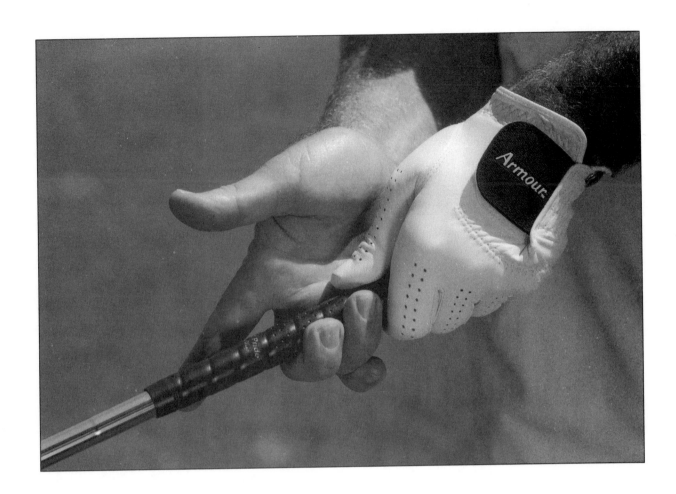

Correction: Grip first with the middle two fingers by laying the shaft in the channel they make when curled. Then lightly close the fingers.

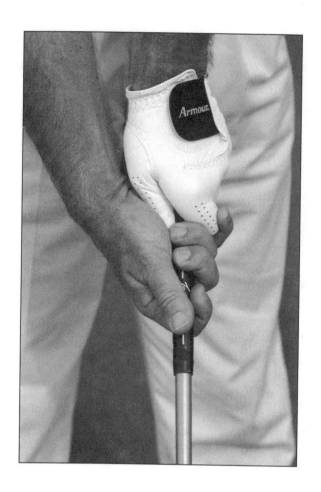 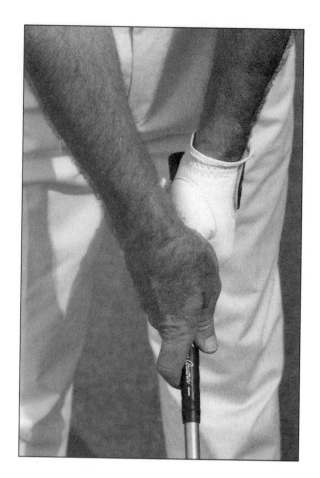

V Formation

Mistake: In this example the hands are rotated too far clockwise, so that the Vs formed by the thumbs and index fingers point to the right of the right shoulder. This tends to close the clubface and encourages a hook.

Mistake: Here the hands are rotated too far counterclockwise, so the Vs made by the thumb and index finger of each hand point to the left of the chin. This tends to open the face and encourages a slice.

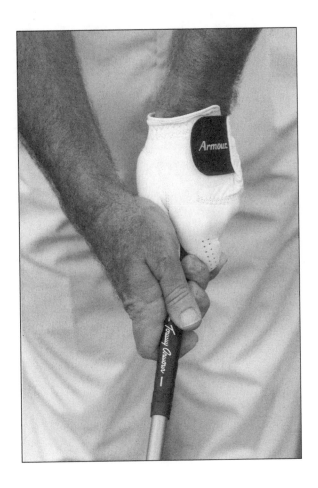

Correction: The Vs of both hands should point somewhere between the right shoulder and the chin. When the left arm is extended and the right hand is facing the target, find your natural arm-hang position. The right-hand grip should be in the fingers and the left-hand grip in the base of the fingers, with the last three fingers in control.

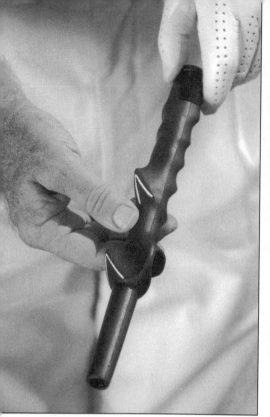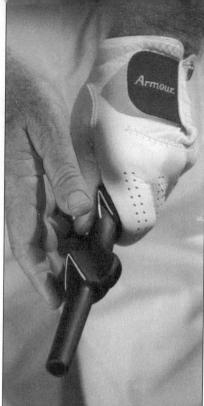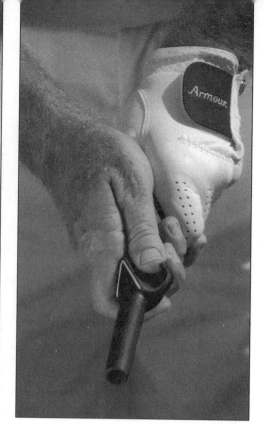

Correction: A formed grip can make correct gripping much easier to master.

Open Face

Mistake: Soling the club with the face open encourages a slice and shots that go high and to the right.

Closed Face

Mistake: Soling the club with the face closed encourages a hook and shots that go low and to the left.

Correction: The leading edge of the clubface should point away from you at a right angle to the target.

The Swing

A golf swing is exactly that—a swing. Frequently in my clinics I will hold up a club and ask what it is. The answer: "A golf club." Next I will ask, "What are you going to try to do with it?" The most frequent response: "Hit the ball."

Wrong! That's the problem—trying to *hit* the ball. You should be trying to *swing the club*.

Of course you hit the ball. But hitting implies force, and the attempt to produce force tends to create tension that destroys a swing. On the other hand, swinging with speed and accuracy has a feeling of lightness rather than tightness.

There are thousands of details to consider in attempting to swing a golf club

effectively. If you try to think your way through them during the course of a swing, you won't make a swing at all. What you will make is a series of unnatural movements totally lacking the blend of grace and energy that characterizes a proficient player's motion. So keep this in mind: a golf swing is made by *feel*. Pay attention to detail prior to initiating the motion, but when the motion begins, rely on a mental picture or be thinking of a single swing key. Never try to think your way through the swing ("head down, arm straight, shift my weight, etc.").

How do you develop this feeling of a good golf swing? First, you must have a precise concept of your goal—a well-executed swing. A professional teacher can be an effective model and guide at this stage.

Next, you must practice so that the concept becomes a feeling. That feeling is sometimes called *muscle memory*, which is a simple way to describe a phenomenon known as motor skill learning. This learning can be enhanced by drills selected to teach specific patterns in the swing. The drills can include hitting balls or just swinging a club, as long as you understand what you are trying to achieve.

Through practice and "overlearning" the basic mechanics of a swing, you can develop trust in the results. Then the challenges of the course and other competitors will not distract you from doing what you know you can do. Practice alone does not make perfect; it only makes permanent. What you practice makes all the difference in the world: practice a swing, not a hit.

An Inside Takeaway

Mistake: While using a flagstick as a reference line, you can monitor your backswing takeaway. A severe inside takeaway on the backswing encourages a reverse weight shift and looping action, causing the club to be cast from outside the intended swing path on the forward swing.

An Outside Takeaway

Mistake: An exaggerated outside takeaway on the backswing encourages a body sway to the right, a high lifting action in the backswing, and a reverse inside loop coming forward.

Correction: Start the club back by pushing it with your left side, letting the clubhead make its natural arc with the left arm as the radius.

Picking the Club Up

Mistake: Picking the club up early produces a backswing that does not properly coil the upper body. It provides only the limited power available from the hands and arms without using the stronger muscles of the back and trunk.

Raising the Head

Mistake: Raising the head and body so the swing center is farther away from the ball than at address makes it very difficult to consistently return the clubface squarely to the ball.

Bent Arm

Mistake: A bent left arm allows the backswing to be almost parallel with the ground, but the shoulders are not properly turned. The upper body is not adequately wound up, so it cannot contribute much power. The left arm also needs more extension in the backswing to get a greater arc for consistency and power.

Correction: At the top of the driver swing the club should be parallel with the ground and the left arm extended but not rigid. The upper body is wound for power, with the head rotated but not raised. In addition, the upper body is aligned over the right leg. The left wrist is flat or nearly so, and the left heel may be slightly off the ground.

Incorrect Weight Shift

Mistake: Here is what a reverse weight shift looks like. The upper part of the body should be over the right leg, not hanging to the left. A reverse weight shift is usually caused by trying to keep the head down rather than allowing it to rotate and move slightly behind the ball. The result of the reverse weight shift is a falling back on the right foot during the forward swing, a bad swing path, and an early hit from the top of the backswing.

Mistake: This is a lower-body reverse weight shift: the lower half of the body goes forward while the upper half shifts back. When the lower body is in a reversed position on the backswing, the weight tends to go back to the right in the downswing, which, of course, is the wrong direction. On the backswing the lower and upper body weight should be over the right leg, not reversed over the left.

Correction: The upper body winds over the right leg on the backswing.

Correct Weight-Shift Drill

Correction: One way to correct a reverse weight shift and improve weight transfer is to practice raising the left leg in the air during the backswing. Look again at the photo on page 26. Note that most of the upper-body weight is over the right leg.

Correction: Continue the swing forward until the right leg leaves the ground. Let the arms hang naturally, grip lightly, and let the momentum of the weight shift provide the power rather than trying to hit with the arms and hands.

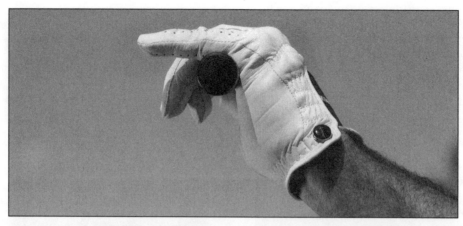

Loss of Club Control

Mistake: Relaxing the last three fingers of your left hand at the top of the backswing will cause you to lose control of the club.

Correction: Hold the club snugly with those last three fingers without squeezing it too tightly.

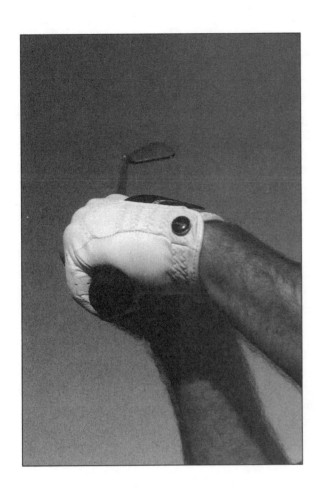 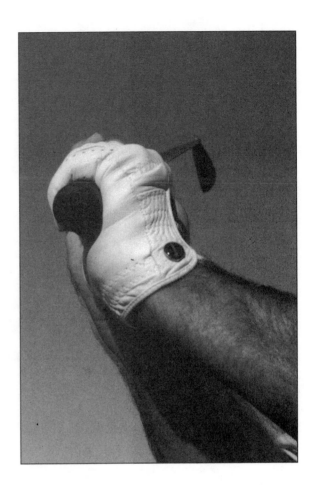

Top of the Backswing

Arched Wrist

Mistake: The left wrist is in an arched position; this is known as *laying the club off*. An arched left wrist at the top of the swing closes the clubface and encourages a hook.

Cupped Wrist

Mistake: At the top of the swing the left wrist is one of the controlling factors in the clubface position. The cupped wrist shown here produces an open clubface (toe pointed to the ground) and encourages a slice.

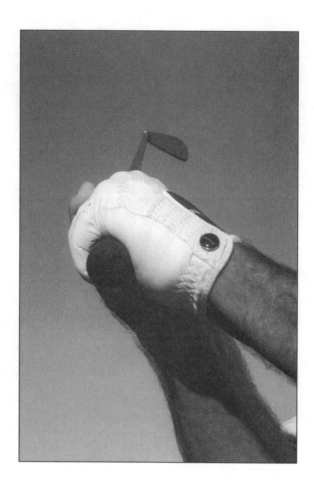

Correction: When the left wrist at the top of the swing is on a plane with the back of the arm, it is in position to produce the most consistent result. From this position it is much easier to return to the ball with the clubface square.

Controlling the Swing Center

Starting from a centered position with the reference pole in the back . . .

Mistake: The center of the swing (at the top of your spine) has drifted too far to the right.

Mistake: The center of the swing has passed where the ball would be located before impact.

Correction: In the impact position the swing center remains slightly behind where the ball would be positioned.

Crowding the Ball

Mistake: Crowding the shot will cause you either to hit behind the ball or bend your arms at impact and lose clubhead speed. While the golfer's position may look correct in the photo, the arms are not at full extension at address and will extend during the swing, causing the clubhead to be lower and to hit the turf behind the ball.

Reaching for the Ball

Mistake: Reaching for the ball produces an erratic swing path, poor balance, and shots that go both to the left and right. It also partially disconnects your arms from the rotational power of your body.

The Setup

Correction: Adjust your grip, bring your arms down until you feel pressure on your chest.

Correction: Bend forward at the hips, soling the club. . . .

Correction: . . . Now adjust your feet.

The Address

Mistake: As shown the hands are too far back, encouraging an outside takeaway.

Mistake: Here the hands are pushed too far forward, encouraging the takeaway to be too far inside.

Addressing with an Iron

Correction: In the proper address position for the iron, the hands will lead the clubhead at address, and the player's head will be more over the ball than behind it.

Addressing with a Wood

Correction: A good address position for the tee shot is with the ball played somewhere between the left shoulder and the left ear. The upper-body weight is slightly behind the ball, perhaps 60 percent to the right, and 40 percent to the left. The lower-body weight is more evenly balanced. The shoulders are parallel to the flight line.

Shanking the Ball

Mistake: Shanking most commonly occurs when the hosel of an iron club makes contact with the ball from an outside-to-in swing path.

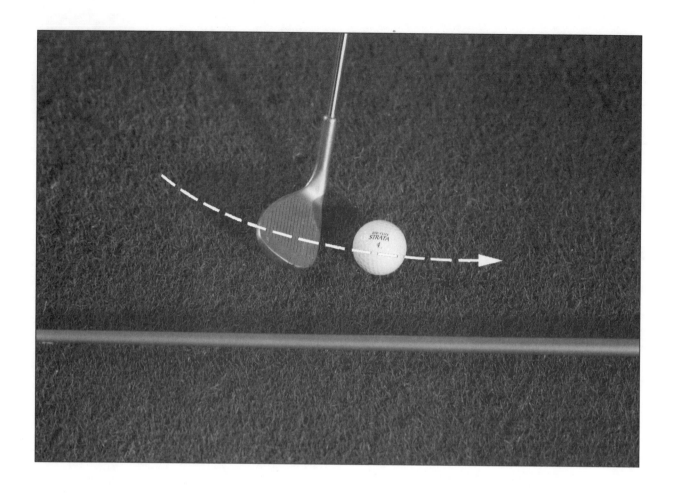

Correction: Swinging along a path that approaches the ball from slightly inside will put the center of the clubface on the ball. Do this by using your lower-body action more to swing the arms than prematurely casting with the hands.

Aiming to the Left

Mistake: Aiming too far to the left encourages the swing to go in that direction, cutting across the target line. This action can produce a slice, a pulled shot, or a pulled hook, depending on the clubface's position.

Aiming to the Right

Mistake: Approximately 80 percent of high-handicap players aim to the right, thinking they are on target because their left shoulder points to it. The result is an attempt to bring the ball back on track by throwing the hands from the top, steep, outside, and across the target line to the left. This action causes pulls, slices, and a loss of distance.

An Aim Routine

Correction: With a club as a pointer, check your shoulder and hip lines to see that they are parallel to a spot left of the target. . . .

Correction: . . . Now complete your setup routine.[1]

[1]The author swung the club after this picture was taken and the ball went right to the flag, stopping inches short from going in. Aim is important!

The Power Path

Correction: This photo illustrates the power path in golf: the swing comes from the inside of the target line to the ball, down the target line, and back to the inside again.

 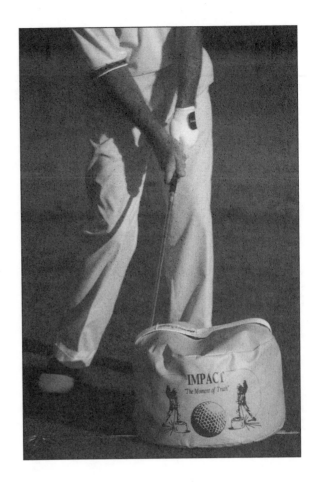

Impact Position

Correction: The correct path is from the inside, and the correct impact position is pictured here. There is only one moment of truth in the golf swing—impact, when the clubface meets the ball. Here I'm using an Impact Bag[2] to teach the correct feeling.

[2]Impact Bag and any other training devices used in this book are available from Golf Around the World, The Training Aids Company: 800-824-4279 or www.golfaroundtheworld.com

The back of the left wrist is flat, not broken down, and the right hand has not passed the left. This practice aid is the best I've ever used for transmitting the feeling of golf's most critical position. I strongly recommend it.

The Full Swing

Here is the full swing sequence for a tee shot.

Address

Address the ball left of center between the left ear and shoulder.

Backswing

Start the club away by a push, keeping your left arm extended, supported by the right hand.

Just past the right hip the hands begin to cock so that by the time the left arm is horizontal the club will be nearly vertical.

Top of the Swing

At the top of the backswing, the club is parallel or nearly parallel with the ground and the left arm is still extended, though not necessarily straight. The upper-body weight is over the right leg. The back slopes away from the target, and the left wrist is either flat or slightly cupped.

Downswing

In the beginning of the downswing, the weight shifts over to the left side, and the hands and arms drop from the over-the-shoulder position to one that comes from the inside. The wrist is still cocked, and the nearly 90-degree angle of the left arm and club is maintained.

The right elbow comes to the right front pocket as the left hip clears out of the way. In this position the arms can swing aggressively through the shot.

Impact and Follow-Through

The arms are extended at impact, and the left wrist is flat.

Halfway into the follow-through, the left elbow has begun to fold, allowing the left hand to rotate and the right arm to extend in a "shaking hands" position. The last three fingers of the left hand are snug around the grip.

The Finish

A good swing is evidenced by a strong finish: in balance, club behind the head, arms comfortable and over the shoulder, weight fully to the left.

3

Around the Green

The best golfers in the world do not hit all 18 greens in regulation figures. Most amateur golfers hit fewer than a third of them during a round. That means there are lots of opportunities for pros and amateurs alike to use those little shots around the green—the chip, the pitch, and the bunker shot. Working on these three skills, combined with improved putting, will lower scores faster than any other investment of practice time. Developing your short game will add confidence to your longer shots, since the consequences of missing a green diminish when you are confident that you can get the ball up and down in two strokes.

Whenever we hit a golf shot, even short shots around the green, there is a tendency to tighten and hit *to* the ball rather than *through* it. A true swing will not slow as it approaches the ball; nor will it stop abruptly at contact. The swinging motion in a short shot should accelerate through the shot. The follow-through should be approximately the same length as the backstroke—a movement not unlike that of a playground swing. In a badly executed short shot, the player either makes a backswing that is too long and tries to decelerate or swings too short and rushes it to hit harder.

One difference between the short-game swing and the full swing is in the grip position. For a chip or short pitch, very little velocity is needed. The hands should be placed lower on the grip; this provides better control. Make these types of shots with little or no wrist cock in the backswing. The motion should be like a pendulum stroke, as it is in putting.

As the length of the shot begins to exceed that of a short chip or pitch, gradually add wrist cock for greater speed without greater effort. A swing with the wrists cocked is often called a *two-lever swing*; a shorter swing with no wrist cock, like the chip or putt, is called a *one-lever swing*.

Chipping and Pitching

The chip and pitch shots are miniature swings with an altered body position at address. Proper club selection enhances your chance of hitting a good shot. It takes greater skill to play a more lofted club, because the margin of error is smaller if you mishit the shot. A good rule to follow is to run the ball when you can, loft it when you have to. Remember when playing pitches and chips that loft is built into the club. You need never feel that you have to lift the shot, only that you need to get the clubface on the ball. So choose the correct club, set up so that the club will be descending on the ball, and swing forward.

Another difference that is critical for successful short shots is the setup. For all

chip shots the centerline of the body run-
ning from your nose downward should be
ahead (to the left of the ball) in the
address. The hands are in line with the
left thigh and the ball in the center of
your stance. This setup encourages a
slight descent on the forward swing,
which assures that the ball will get on the

center of the clubface. In the chip the feet
are closer together than in a full shot,
with the left foot drawn back to open the
body more to the target. The open stance
position allows the backswing to be more
on the target line rather than being taken
inside.

Too Much Loft

Mistake: The most frequent chipping error comes in selecting a club with too much loft when loft is not needed. Here, for example, the player selects a sand wedge for a shot from just off the green where that much loft isn't needed.

Correction: For this shot use a more straight-bladed club, in this case an 8-iron, and stroke the ball like a putt but with a little clubhead descent. Also, if the grass allows, you can choose to putt from off the green. This choice is generally the safest.

Setup Mistake

Mistake: Here the player is trying to chip with the hands over, or worse, behind the ball and the head to the right of it.

Correction: Play the shot with the hands ahead of the ball, the shaft angle leaning forward, ball position back of center, and the head over the ball or slightly forward of it to improve consistency.

Scooping the Ball

Mistake: Attempting to lift the shot by scooping the ball in the air is the most common cause of hitting behind a pitch shot or blading the ball across the green.

Correction: Set the shaft angled forward, keeping the hands ahead of the clubhead. Instead of trying to lift the ball, let the clubhead descend so the loft in the clubface can lift it.

Correction: Keep the back of the left hand flat by not letting the clubhead pass your hands.

Picture-Perfect Golf

The Pitch from Heavy Rough

Mistake: Trying to pitch the ball from heavy rough with a normal low backswing results in too much grass getting between the blade and the ball.

Correction: Make a steeper backswing when the ball is down in the heavy rough, so that the angle of descent will be greater, and the clubface will not catch up in the grass. Use a sand wedge for this shot.

The Bunker Shot

The bunker swing is almost always a two-lever swing with the wrists cocking more abruptly than usual. The shot out of the sand with the ball sitting on the surface does not differ a great deal from a pitch shot from the grass over a bunker. The major change is the ball position. The ball should be played more forward in the stance in order to hit the sand—not the ball. Remember, do not hit the sand and

stop. Finish your swing—the way it is illustrated in the photographs in this chapter.

When you don't know how to play a shot from a sand bunker, it is one of the hardest shots in golf; when you do, it is one of the easiest.

Play the shot with the club made specifically for that situation, the sand wedge. The execution of the shot when the ball is resting on top of the sand is as follows:

1. Move the ball forward in your stance in line with your left eye.
2. Cock your wrists more abruptly so that you'll get more descent.
3. Open the clubface slightly to help guarantee bounce and to avoid digging with the sole of the club.
4. Aim to the left of the target with your stance to offset the open face position. Let the swing travel parallel to your shoulder line, left of your target, so that you are hitting a cut shot.
5. Finish the swing so the hands get shoulder high. This will promote acceleration.
6. When the ball is buried, move it back in your stance, square the clubface, and descend steeply. The follow-through is less important.

A few practice sessions in the bunker working on the correct mechanics can reduce any anxiety about playing from the sand.

Poor Footing

Mistake: Here the feet are not dug into the sand. On a long bunker shot with more effort in the swing, the feet will not hold their position. This can cause the player to slide and mishit the shot.

Correction: Work the feet down into the sand to get a more stable base and shorten your grip length to offset the lower position of your feet.

Hands Behind the Ball

Mistake: Setting the hands behind the ball encourages the average player to level out the swing at the bottom too quickly and bounce the club off the sand and into the ball rather than cut beneath it.

Correction: The hands should be even with the ball, as shown here, or, better, ahead in a normal pitch-shot position. This position will improve the angle of attack, provide a more descending blow, and cut the sand from underneath the ball.

Around the Green

Buried Lie

If the ball is buried, however, the player should set up differently.

Correction: Place the ball farther back toward the right in the stance so that the hands are ahead of the clubhead. Do not open the blade, but allow the leading edge to turn downward so it will dig rather than bounce. Allow for considerably more roll when the ball lands on the green.

The Bunker Chip

Mistake: A chip shot out of a bunker is a very difficult shot to play. Even the tour player rarely uses it. While it may not technically be a mistake, it's a low-percentage shot.

Correction: A fuller "splash" swing makes a bunker shot much easier once you learn it . . . so learn it!

Deceleration

Mistake: Decelerating near impact is one of the most common mistakes in bunker play and causes the ball to stay in the bunker. Note the lack of follow-through.

Correction: Swing the club to a more complete finish, shifting your weight from the right foot to the left. The length of the follow-through should be at least equal to that of the backswing. In a short bunker shot the backswing and follow-through may not be as extended as the follow-through shown here.

The Short, Low Backswing

Mistake: A backswing that is too low and too short will not allow the clubhead to descend properly. The result will be a lifting action that strikes the ball without taking enough sand (sometimes none at all) blading the shot out of the bunker and across the green.

Correction: Cock the wrists more quickly or swing the arms upward more than normal in the takeaway to get the club in position to make a better descent on the downswing.

Uphill Lie

Mistake: Normally it is correct to match the shoulder level with the ground slope. But some uphill lies are too steep to allow this to work. When this happens, the player leans too far to the right and hits behind the ball.

Correction: One answer is to lean into the hill and hit closer behind the ball without attempting to follow through.

Downhill Lie

Mistake: With a downhill bunker shot the tendency is to hit too far behind the ball and sail it across the green. This usually happens because the shoulder line is tilted upward and the ground is tilted downward.

Correction: Tilt the shoulders to conform to the level of the ground so that the club will follow its slope down and through, cutting the sand from underneath the ball. The shot should be played a little more toward the right foot in the stance. Allow for the ball to come out lower than normal and with more velocity.

Using a Wood from the Sand

Mistake: Playing a fairway wood from a sand bunker is difficult, particularly if there is an elevated lip in front of you.

Correction: The smart choice for the average player in a fairway bunker is to use an iron. Rule 1: *Get out first.*

Correction: If the ball is sitting up perfectly on top of the sand, however, and you are confident of making the shot, a lofted wood *can* be used. But in most cases, particularly if a lip obstructs the shot, pitch out safely with a more lofted club. Do this by shortening down a bit on the grip and playing the ball back in your stance more than normal. Take a three-quarter swing and catch the ball first, not the sand.

Putting

Willie Park Jr., a famous nineteenth-century Scottish golfer, once said, "The man who can putt is a match for anyone." He was right; and, of course, it goes for women golfers as well.

Putting is almost a game unto itself. No other aspect of golf invites such a diversity of individual styles while, at the same time, requiring such precise execution.

Although variations in equipment and style are more the norm than the exception, a putt is still a swing. Grip lightly, feel the weight of the clubhead, then accelerate *through*, not *to*, the ball. Develop a comfortable routine and repeat it on each putt. This will establish a pattern, build confidence, and reduce tension.

- Stand bent forward at the hips so that the *left eye* is over the ball. By assuming this position, you place your body at the correct distance from the ball so that the natural swing arc of the putter will be neither too far inside your target line nor too far out. In this setup, the ball is also far enough forward so that you stroke it at the bottom of the swing arc or just as the arc is coming up.
- Be positive. The greatest golfers I've ever seen are all supremely confident in their putting ability.
- Visualize the ball rolling across the green toward the target before you hit it, practice stroke to get the feel, and trust the feeling.

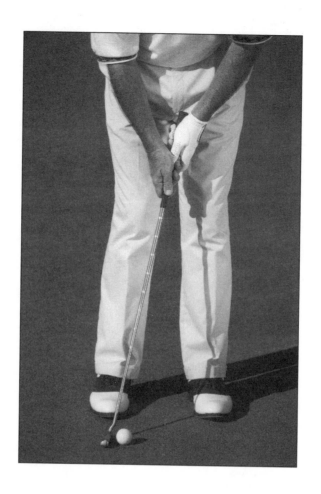

Ball Too Far Back
in the Stance

Mistake: The ball is played too far back in the stance. This causes a descending stroke that makes the ball start with a hop rather than a roll.

Ball Too Far Forward in the Stance

Mistake: When the ball is positioned too far forward, the shaft angle tilts back, adds putter face loft, and tends to cause pulls and left-wrist breakdown.

Correction: Place the ball under the left eye. Let your arms and hands hang naturally, hands over the ball.

Standing Too Close or Too Far

Mistake: By standing too close to the ball in putting you force the backswing outside the takeaway, causing an arc that is too far off line to produce a consistently accurate stroke.

Mistake: Standing too far from the ball causes a stroke path that makes too much of an arc from the inside and allows the face to be square to the target only momentarily.

Correction: Check to get your eyes over the ball by dropping a plumb line from the bridge of your nose to the ball. Then stand that distance away.

Hitting to the Right of the Hole

Mistake: Taking the putter blade too far to the inside early in the backswing encourages a return path from inside to out, with the ball being pushed to the right.

Hitting to the Left of the Hole

Mistake: Taking the putter blade too far to the outside encourages an inside return path so that the ball is pulled to the left of target.

Correction: Taking the blade back down the line for the first few inches makes it easier to return the blade squarely to the target.[1] As the backswing continues, the putter should eventually come inside of the straight line in a natural arc.

[1]To purchase this or any other training aid for golf, contact Golf Around the World, Inc. at 800-824-4279.

Pulling the Ball to the Left

Mistake: Proper alignment is one of golf's most difficult fundamentals to master; it is particularly important for accurate putting. Here the player's body alignment is to the left, encouraging him to pull the ball to the left as well, unless he compensates by blocking out the release and pushing the blade toward the target.

Pushing the Ball to the Right

Mistake: Here the alignment is too far to the right, encouraging a push. The player must swing the clubhead back toward the hole and cut across the line of flight in order to start the ball on the correct path.

Correction: Get the arm and shoulder line parallel to the target line. Aim the face at right angles and use a pendulum stroke.

Accurate Backstrokes

Mistake: A backstroke that is too long for the length of putt causes the putter head to decelerate as it approaches the ball. This mistake is one of the most common to putting and produces very erratic results.

Correction: A shorter backstroke with positive acceleration rolls the ball much more consistently. The backswing, however, should not be so short that the putting motion feels more like hitting than stroking. Move your putter like a pendulum, swinging it back and through.

Golf's Most Common Errors

There are certain mistakes made when trying to hit a golf ball that occur more frequently than others—golf's most common errors. For some players, these problems are perennial; they repeat them over and over, year after year, without ever doing anything substantial to make a change. Yet all problems in golf have solutions—some of which are quite simple. Identifying the cause of the error is the first step toward correction; that step is then followed by the application of the correct solution. The examples in this chapter may help you to eliminate a particular mistake that is frequent enough in your play to be considered a perennial problem.

Topping the Ball

Mistake: Topping the ball is caused by hitting it above its center. In this case the head and center of the swing have been raised from their original positions at address. Raising up is most frequently caused by excessive tension in the arms when trying to hit rather than swing.

Mistake: The head and the center of the swing have been moved back to the right as a result of trying to lift the ball into the air. If the weight stays on the back foot during the forward swing, the club reaches the bottom of its arc too soon and tops the ball or hits behind it. The first move in the forward swing should be to shift your weight to the left side.

Mistake: Bending the left arm at impact raises the clubhead so that the ball is topped even though the head stays down. The left arm must swing through with extension if it's to return to where it was at address. Too much right-hand pressure is a frequent cause of the left arm's bending.

Mistake: If the ball position is too far forward in the address, the clubhead will reach the bottom of its arc too soon and will catch the ball on top.

Stopping the Topping

Correction: Here the swing center has not been raised in the backswing, and the arms maintain arc width. The shoulders and hands will return relaxed as the weight shifts to the left. . . .

Correction: . . . When the previous moves happen, you will take a divot or at least scrape a little grass from a spot forward of the ball's original position.

Incorrect Ball Impact

Mistake: Impacting the ball in the heel of the clubface results in a fade and lost distance. Usually this result is caused by hitting too early with the hands in the forward swing and casting the clubhead path outside of the flight line.

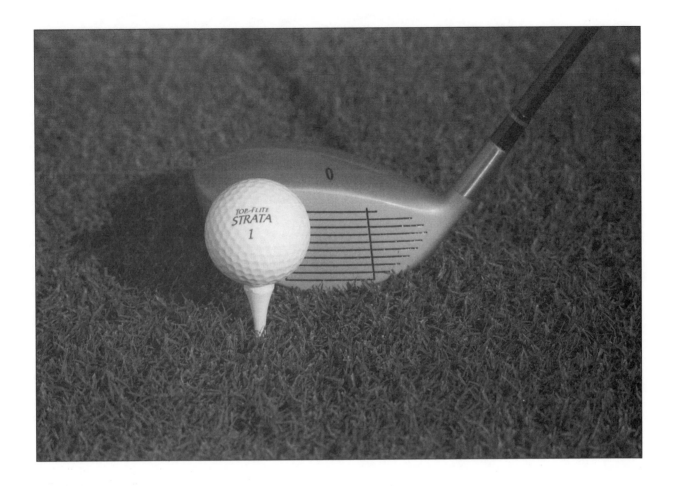

Mistake: Impacting the ball on the toe creates a toe hook and lost distance. This result is caused either by tension in the arms that pulls the club inward or by standing too far from the ball.

Correction: Center face contact causes the ball to go both farther and straighter. It comes most often from a relaxed swinging motion.

Hitting Behind the Ball

Mistake: Hitting behind the ball—a fat shot—is the result of the clubhead arriving out of sequence, before the weight shift to the left side and the forward arm swing have been completed. It is evident in this picture that the weight has not been shifted to the left side.

Mistake: Playing the ball too far forward in the stance can cause you to hit the ground before the ball.

Correcting the Fat Shot

Correction: Place a tee in the ground to mark the location of the back of the ball, i.e., the first point of contact. Then . . .

When you make a full swing and release the right foot so the heel-to-toe line is vertical, the divot will come out *after* the ball has been struck. Note the divot ahead of the tee. An effective five-word slogan for your practice swing and shot is "*Grass ahead of the ball.*"

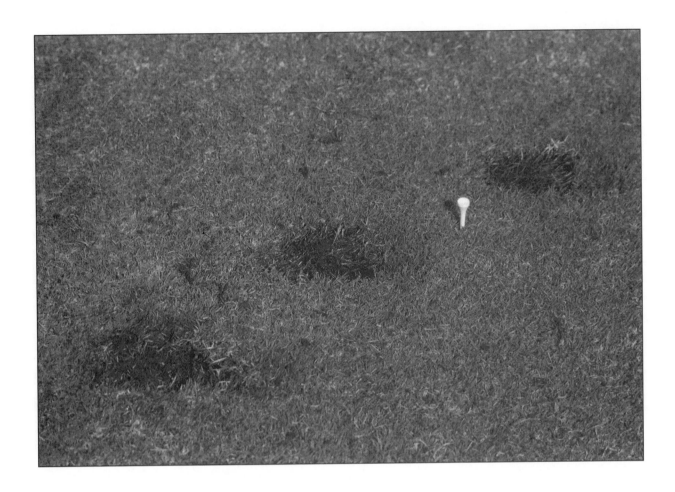

Correction: This picture shows the result of three different swings. Imagine a ball placed just forward, above, and to the right of the tee. With the swing traveling from left to right across the page the divot farthest to the left demonstrates a swing made with the weight remaining on the right side. The middle divot shows a partial weight transfer. The divot to the right shows the correct weight transfer.

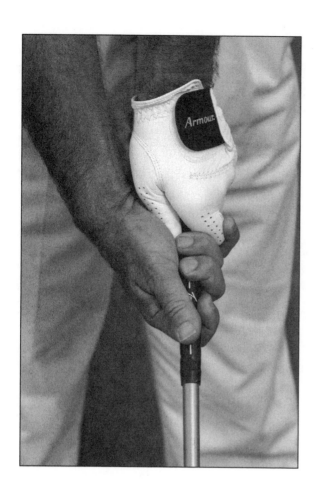

Common Errors That Cause You to Hook the Ball

Mistake: In this grip position the hands are rotated too far under—clockwise when looking down. This type of grip—called a "strong grip" or "closed-faced grip"—encourages a closed clubface.

Mistake: Rolling the right forearm excessively to close the clubface.

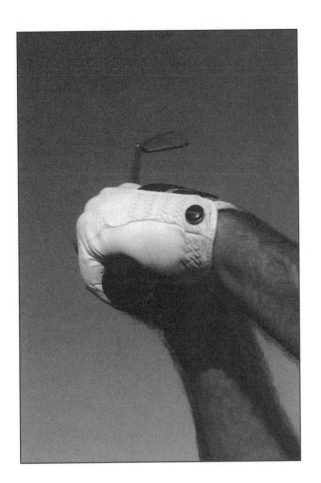 

Mistake: The face is shut because of the arched left-wrist position at the top of the backswing.

Mistake: The player's weight is back on the right foot, encouraging a swing path to the left with a closing clubface.

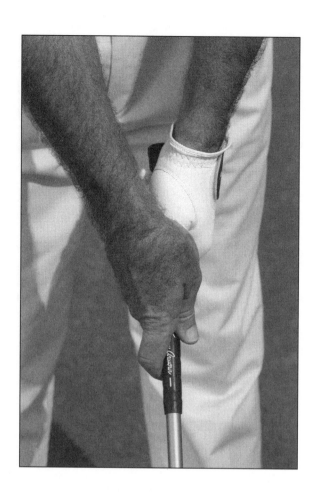 

Common Errors That Cause You to Slice the Ball

Mistake: This grip position of the hands is rotated too far on top—counterclockwise when looking down. It encourages an open clubface and is known as a "weak grip" or "open face grip."

Mistake: Here the weight is too far left, moving the swing center past the ball, which causes the clubface to remain open.

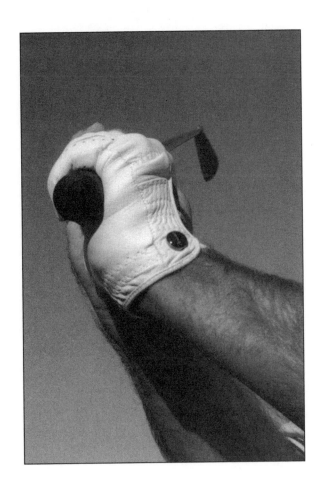

Mistake: The left wrist is excessively cupped at the top of the backswing, and the clubface is open.

Mistake: Excessive tension in the hands or separation of the left arm from the body blocks the release of the clubface.

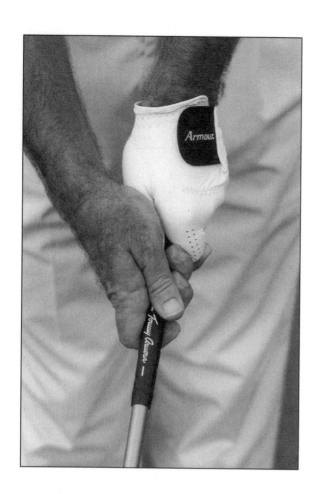 

Correcting the Hook
and the Slice

Correction: Start with a good grip.   **Correction:** Square the takeaway.

Correction: The wrist is flat and the clubface square at the top of the backswing; the clubshaft is parallel to the flight line.

Correction: Impact is with the weight to the left and the back of the left hand toward the target while the swing center is still behind the ball.

Correction: Finish totally left, arms comfortable and the upper body released toward the target.

Picture-Perfect Golf

6

Unusual Lies and Conditions

Golf would be a good game without unusual conditions; with them, it's a great game. Sloping lies, wet days and dry days, windy days and still days, long grass and short grass, deep sand and shallow sand, hot weather and cold weather; greens that are fast and slow, grainy and smooth, hard and soft—a golf course changes not only by the day but sometimes by the hour.

The ability to handle unusual conditions separates the star from the struggler, the champ from the chump. Study experienced golfers (including your course professional) and ask them for tips on handling those out-of-the-ordinary shots.

One of golf's most basic principles is that whenever conditions are not normal, play more conservatively. On sloping lies, for example—above or below the feet, uphill or downhill—it is advisable to take a club that requires less effort and use a more controlled swing. Gravity is the enemy on sloping lies. It is much more difficult to maintain balance when the ball is at a different level or one foot is higher or lower than the other. On an uphill shot the slope also increases the effective loft in your clubface; it may be necessary to select a club or two longer, depending on the severity of the slope.

Remember also that hitting from sloping lies tends to produce different flight patterns. Shots made with the ball resting above or uphill tend to go left; below and downhill slopes tend to shoot the ball right. The easiest way to handle these situations is to anticipate the result of the shot and adjust for it by aiming a compensating distance to allow for the new flight.

Wind is considered a golfer's enemy. But really it's just another challenge; personally, I rather enjoy it. One thing is for sure, though: you'd better learn to hug the ground a bit more with the trajectory of your shots. Wind plays havoc on golf shots with high flight. Remember the principle of trajectory control: *the more you angle the grip end of the club forward (in advance of the clubhead), the lower the shot will travel.* Moving the grip end of the club backward adds loft to the face and height to the trajectory. For a low shot, the standard practice is to move the ball back in the stance. When you do this, the grip end moves forward in relation to the head.

To execute a shot into the wind, select a club one or more club numbers lower for the distance you wish the shot to travel. Shorten your grip down by about two inches. Move the ball back of center in your stance and keep your hands in their normal position. Take a three-quarter-length swing back and make a three-quarter-length finish. Don't try to punch the ball—instead just swing, keeping the relation of your hands and clubhead the same at impact as it was at address.

When attempting to increase the trajectory to go over an obstacle, move the grip end of the club back by placing the ball farther forward in the stance. Be sure to be aggressive with your weight shift and left arm or you will tend to hit behind the ball.

It takes practice to learn all of the little "tricks" or adjustments that are necessary when you face unusual lies and conditions. But doing so can save you from experiencing bad shots on the course.

Ball Above the Feet

Mistake: When the ball is above your feet, it is actually closer to you, and with a full-length grip (as pictured) you'll have a tendency to hit behind the ball. Gravity tries to move the body backward, causing you to pull the shot to the left even when the ball is hit squarely. And finally, when the clubhead is higher than your feet, the face looks to the left.

Correction: Shortening the grip results in a more balanced stance and a swing that clears the ground better. Use a club that is stronger (less loft) by one number to compensate for the loss of distance from the shortened grip. On an uneven lie the swing should always be slightly more controlled than under normal conditions. Aim out to the right, because the ball tends to go left.

Picture-Perfect Golf

Uphill Lie

Mistake: On an uphill slope gravity tugs the body back toward the rear foot and tilts the shoulder line back too much. A swing from this position hits behind the ball, tops it, or pulls it strongly to the left.

Correction: Lean into the hill a bit more to fight the pull of gravity, but keep the shoulders matched with the slope of the hill and aim to the right.

Correction: Make an extra effort to transfer your weight to the left, "fighting" up the hill.

Ball Below the Feet

Mistake: When the ball is below the feet, gravity tends to pull the body forward, and you are likely to heel or shank the shot or, because the ball is lower than normal, top it.

Correction: Stand a little closer to the ball and sit deeply in your knees so that the weight rests more on the heels. Grip the club at the top in order to reach the ball more easily. Aim more to the left, because the lowered club opens the face.

Picture-Perfect Golf

Downhill Lie

Mistake: Do not tilt the shoulder upward and put the center of the body too far behind the ball when playing a downhill lie. A swing from this position tops the ball, hits badly behind it, or skulls the shot.

Correction: Put the shoulders in a position that better matches the slope of the ground and moves the center of the body toward the left. The follow-through should match the contour of the ground.

The Rules of Golf

Do you know of any other game with 23 million participants (in the United States alone) in which less than 1 percent of them know the rules contained in a book of a little over 120 pages? It's not that the rules are simple; they couldn't be and cover all the variables of play on sixteen thousand different courses. But the fact is that most golfers have never read the rule book, although it is available in almost any golf shop.

The rules provide conditions under which players may compete fairly. They are meant to be equitable, not punitive. No player should be allowed an advantage over another except by skill. When the rules don't cover a situation, fairness should prevail.

The original 13 rules didn't cover every situation—today there are 34 rules, plus a substantial Appendix. And that's not all: the rule-making bodies, the United States Golf Association and the Royal and Ancient Golf Club of St. Andrews, publish a book of decisions that rivals in thickness an unabridged dictionary. This book chronicles the individual cases that, over the years, led to the establishment of and changes in the rules.

Buy a copy of the rule book and read four pages a night for a month. By doing so, you will join a very select company in the world of golf—those who have read the rules. (*Note*: a two-page etiquette section precedes the rules. From what I've seen on the course, it hasn't been widely read either.)

Soling the Club in a Hazard

Mistake: Soling the club within the confines of a hazard is not allowed. The penalty is two strokes in medal play or loss of hole in match play.

Correction: Suspend the club above the ground; touch the turf only in the course of the swing.

Soling the Club in a Bunker

Mistake: Soling the club in a bunker is a two-stroke penalty in medal play or loss of hole in match play.

Correction: Suspend the club in the air and don't brush the sand on the backswing.

Course Etiquette

Mistake: Do not leave footprints in a bunker—and never climb out on the steep side.

Picture-Perfect Golf

Correction: Always rake the bunker to a smooth condition and leave from the lowest side.

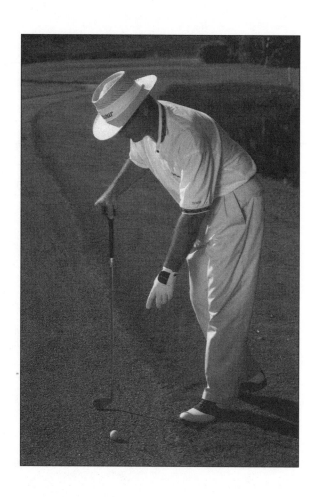

Unplayable Lie

Mistake: This ball has landed on a cart path. Do not measure from the opposite side of the path or closer to the hole. Always find the nearest point of relief that is no closer to the hole.

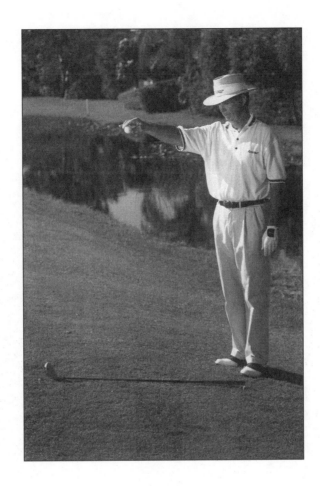

Correction: Place a tee at the nearest point that is not closer to the hole, measure one club length, and drop the ball from shoulder height.

Relief from Movable and Immovable Obstructions

In this picture (left) the ball has come to rest near a tee marker (a movable obstruction). If the marker interferes with my stance or swing, I may move it and replace it after the shot.

In this picture (right) the sprinkler timer box interferes with the swing. You are allowed one club length relief from the condition no nearer to the hole. This relief also applies if any other immovable obstruction interferes with your stance.

Footprints, Loose Impediments, and Movable Obstructions in a Hazard

The ball is in a footprint in a hazard (sand bunker). Relief without penalty is not allowed. The objects to the left of the ball are movable obstructions: a rake, a cup, an empty golf ball sleeve, a pop can, and a golf glove container. If they interfere with the stance or swing in a hazard, the player may remove them. Objects on the right are loose impediments: a stone, a stick, a pinecone, and a leaf. If any of these are in a hazard and interfere with the player's stance or swing, the player is not allowed relief or permitted to move them unless they cover the ball entirely from sight.

CHAPTER
7

Tips for the Smart Golfer

The term *course management* has come into vogue in the past few years, replacing *playing smart* or *playing stupid*—although the latter phrases are more descriptive. What has to be managed? Two things—judgment and emotions. Course management includes psychological control as well as strategy.

There are a growing number of golf specialists who deal solely in the field of psychology. This book touches only lightly on the psychological aspects of golf; for a more in-depth treatment of this subject, read *Your Personal Golf Mental Trainer*, or *Your Personal Golf Course Management Trainer*, available from Golf Around the World (1-800-824-4279).

Believe in yourself as a golfer. Don't dwell on your shortcomings. Convince yourself you can succeed. Fear, doubt, hesitancy, uncertainty, and indecision all lead to failure in golf.

You wouldn't be human if you didn't feel some nervousness under pressure. Champions develop strategies to reduce fear so that it doesn't keep them from performing up to their capabilities. For example: 1. put the experience in perspective; 2. occupy the mind with procedure to avoid dwelling on consequences of a bad shot; or 3. concentrate on images of past successes.

Anger is a self-defeating response in golf. It produces muscle tension and reduces the ability to think. It can be useful if it motivates you by becoming angry enough to practice, but golfers normally should maintain an inner calm and not become angry.

Strategy, tactics, and smart play are a part of course management. Although I'm a long hitter, I've taken my share of drubbings from players whose drives I've surpassed by 25 to 50 yards. So I can personally attest to the superior wisdom of being a smart player rather than a long hitter.

Playing smart means

1. not automatically using a driver because the hole is a par 4 or par 5 (Some holes call for a shorter tee shot to be safe or a particularly straight tee shot that might not be easily made with a driver.)

2. selecting a club that allows you to make a comfortable swing

3. choosing a club with less loft for playing into the wind and uphill; choosing one with more loft for playing with the wind and downhill

4. playing to the safe part of the green when the pin is in a precarious place that allows little margin for error

5. teeing the ball close to the side of trouble so you can aim away from it

6. not pressing for extra distance when playing into a stiff wind

Playing golf intelligently, using the best odds, and taking the least risk will reduce your number of "disaster" holes. You don't have to be smart to play smart golf; you have to be sensible. I would bet that Jack Nicklaus used his 3-wood from the tee instead of his driver more often than any other modern PGA Tour player. I'd say he's a pretty smart golfer.

Determining Your Correct Distance

On par-3 holes check the permanent marker for the distance to the center of the green. The tee markers, however, may be several yards ahead or behind the distance marker. Walk off the distance from the tee blocks to the permanent marker to determine your distance to the middle of the green, either adding or subtracting. Then take into account the flagstick location. Greens that are exceptionally deep from front to back can easily require a three-club difference according to the flagstick location. Finally, judge the wind to make your final calculation of "actual playing yardage," not scorecard yardage.

Pressing for Distance

Mistake: On long holes such as this, don't strain for extra distance. The effort will only create tension, which destroys a good swing motion.

Correction: Make your normal effort and your best swing especially on long holes or when playing with long hitters. The test is, "Did you finish in balance?"

Teeing Up the Ball Near a Water Hazard

Mistake: The ball is teed up on the wrong side of the tee ground. This location encourages the player to aim toward the water hazard.

Correction: Tee the ball up closer to the hazard and drive the ball away from the primary trouble spot, not toward it.

Getting Out of Trouble

Mistake: When trying to recover from trouble (particularly in loose dirt, loose sand, or pine needles), don't expect miracle-distance full shots. Also, don't position the ball too far forward if you do decide to chip out.

Correction: Play the ball back toward the right foot, and pitch to safety. From this setup position there is less chance of hitting the ground first.

Preparing for Competition

A player in competition should be prepared for all eventualities. Towels, extra gloves, umbrella, rain suit, and a light slipover windbreaker are critical. If a player can't keep the grips dry, he or she will lose total control of the club. Extra shoes help if you are playing 36 holes that day or if the tournament lasts more than one day.

Developing a Routine
for Consistency

The most difficult task for golfers at any level is to produce consistent golf shots. To develop consistency, find a workable pattern or routine to follow. The following pages offer a sample golf routine—from start to finish.

Routine: Assess the lie to determine club selection and the type of shot.

Determine the yardage to the flagstick or to whatever location you intend to play. Determining yardage may be done with the assistance of yardage markers, a yardage book, a range finder, a scorecard, or notes you've taken previously. And, of course, it can be done visually. Include checking the wind as part of your routine.

Picture-Perfect Golf

Visualize the shot. Visualization is a very important part of making consistent golf shots. *See* it before you *do* it.

Select the correct club based on your observations and feelings.

Picture-Perfect Golf

Aim from behind, drawing an imaginary line from the flag to the ball, and approach from the rear.

Grip the club and assess the distance from the ball by measuring with your left arm against your chest, walking into the stance.

Sole the club, feeling your left arm on your chest.

While taking the address position, stay in motion by using a waggle. Don't let tension build up in your body.

Swing to the top.

Swing through to the finish.

Evaluate the result. If it was good, savor it and imprint it in your memory. If it was poor, take a practice swing the way it should have been done and visualize the desired result.

Picture-Perfect Golf

Final Bits of Advice

We hope you have enjoyed and profited from this pictorial trip through the challenges presented in trying to master the game of golf. While you'll never quite reach perfection, much of the joy comes from trying to improve and finding those moments when you do.

1. Visual study as presented in this book is an effective way to enhance learning and performance of a motor skill like golf. Review the pictures, compare them with others in golf magazines and books, then look at yourself in a mirror, on video, or in photos.

2. Share information and thoughts with your golf professional so that you develop a trained, objective eye to help you sort out the correct from the incorrect. Doing so will help make the game easier and your scores lower.

3. There is no improvement without practice. It can be physical or mental, but it must happen, and it must be correct. That's the reason for this book.

4. Take care of your body so that even as a super-senior, as I am in this picture, you can enjoy your golf.

Index